20

Internal Quality Assurance
Verifier Award

This document will demonstrate the knowledge in Understanding the context and principles of IQ, The Understanding of how to plan the IQA of assessment, the Understanding of the techniques and criteria for monitoring the quality of internal assessment, the Understanding of how to maintain and improve the quality of assessment, the understanding of how to manage information relevant to the IQA of assessment and understand the legal and best practice requirements for the IQA of assessment.

Tina A Smith

Microsoft

1/1/2016

IQA

VERIFIER AWARD

BY TINA A SMITH

Unit T/601/5320 – level 4

1.1 The functions of IQA in learning and development

It is the role of the IQA (Internal Quality Assessor) to monitor and evaluate the Assessors competency in delivering teaching, assessment and development planning to the learner to cover the criteria of the qualifications being undertaken. IQA supports this by ensuring learner employees and employers are aware of the role the qualification will play in improving their business via understanding policies and procedures. This is under taken by visits to employers and employees on site assessing and agreeing, forward planning actions and development.

IQA ensure the quality of evidence gathered and submitted in all qualifications. The delivery and assessment methods are given constructive feedback to assessors on this evidence. The IQA is checking that the evidence is reliable and authentic using a variety of assessment methods that comply with the (NOS) National Occupational Standards as described by the Sector Skills Council and described in the assessment strategy.

Following on from this the IQA will ensure that assessors are compliant with the assessment

strategy and all evidence submitted is VACS (Valid, Authentic, Current and Sufficient).
The IQA will create, hold and update the IQA file in which the sampling plan of students work is planned and identified. The sampling plan will identify when an assessors work will be required to be available to the IQA for interim or end sampling.   This is where assessor feedback is stored along with copies of the assessor's qualifications and CV.

IQA's run standardisation meetings which are to ensure that the assessors within a team are accurate and consistent in their decisions and that they are consistent in their interpretation of standards and outcome criteria for the qualification. The IQA is also available to assessors to support, agree and standardise the interpretation of standards.

Part of the IQA role is to assess and manage risk. Risk can be health and safety on site, safety of the employee when working and identify any issues or trends, to ensure the learner journey is quality and training and development has taken place.

The IQA also is responsible for upholding the credibility of the qualification being assessed, ensuring the accuracy and consistency in decisions. As well as ensuring all assessors have up to date and continuing CPD and that procedures are monitored and evaluated continuously to identify and improvements, which should then be implemented immediately.

Ann Gravell (www.anngravell.co.uk) states that, "If there is no external formal examination taken by learners, there has to be a system of monitoring the performance of assessors. If not, assessors might make incorrect judgments or pass someone who hasn't met the requirements because they were biased towards them."

1.2 The key concepts and principles of the IQA of assessment

The IQA is responsible for the monitoring of the learner journey to ensure they have received a quality service and that assessment is fair and correct. The process involves planning what will be monitored, from whom and when. To observe training, planning, teaching and learning has taken place within assessor practices and give developmental feedback that is constructive.
The process also involves meeting with the learners, their managers and any witnesses. IQA are also responsible for facilitating the standardisation process of assessor practices, holding team meetings and supporting assessors.

The key concepts of IQA include:
VACSR
Assessment strategies
Evaluation
Accountability (to your organisation and any
external bodies)
Risk factors
Formative and summative sampling
Having a rationale

Valid – the methods used were in line with the
criteria needed to meet the standards for that
qualification, they were used appropriately and in
context.
Authentic – the methods used were ethical, there
has been no plagiarism, the work submitted is that
of the learner and authentic.
Current – the work submitted is in real time and
real working environment and not simulated.
Safe – the methods used were at the level required,
and took into account the learners needs, also that
the methods used were based on the requirements
of the criteria, planned and feedback was given.
Learning and assessment was not compromised,
confidentiality was taken into account and that the
learner experience is quality and has the potential
to achieve.
Reliable – A decision was made that was not bias,
and in line with similar decisions made with similar
learners working at the same level.

Assessment Strategies, Evaluation and having a rationale –

A good IQA system will start with a rationale. This is the reason why IQA takes place and ensures the activities used are safe, valid, fair and reliable. (Ann Gravell – www.anngravell.co.uk)
The IQA plan is then written up to formalise what will be carried out and when, ensuring that assessment decisions are carried out by qualified assessors, sampled by qualified internal quality assurers to ensure the fairness, safety, validity and reliability of assessment methods and decisions. This in turn will uphold the credibility of the qualification and reputation of the organisation. IQA will also provide continuing support for the assessor and learner by regular contact. IQA will sample units as per rationale, observe practice (at least once a year) and interview learners about their experience using set questions.
Dylan William (The journey to Excellence) - http://www.journeytoexcellence.org.uk/videos/expertspeakers/assessmentstrategiesdylanwiliamtrans.asp

If we take the three central processes in assessments of making sure that: you are clear about where the learner is going; you are clear about where they are and you want to establish how to get there; and you think about the role of the teacher; the role of the other peers in the classroom and the learner themselves. You end up with five, what we call - key strategies.

The first is the teacher's role in making sure that you know where the learner is through questioning, classroom tasks, dialogue - it's finding out where the learner is. Then giving feedback to the students and not feedback that tells them they are doing okay and no they are not doing okay, but it's feedback that moves the learner forward. Then you have the role of peer, first of all helping each other understand success criteria. The teacher helps clarify what the lesson is about and what the learning is about and peers have a role in communicating this to each other as well. You have peers supporting each other - what we call activating students as teaching resources of one another. You have student self-assessment or activating students as owners of their own learning. That brings in all the stuff about metacognition; managing all your emotional reaction to school and to work. We get this complex of ultimately five processes.

There is a question in finding out where students are within their learning; the feedback that moves learners; making sure that everybody concerned is clear about the success criteria; student peer assessment and student self-assessment. Those we think are the five key processes or five key strategies for Assessment for Learning. Some which so... that we would say that if you are doing Assessment for Learning you are doing at least one of those - and if you are not doing one of those then you are not doing Assessment for Learning.

Accountability and risk factors –
You have to be accountable to your company and the awarding bodies as well as other external bodies, within an organization, the principles and practices of ethical accountability aim to improve both the internal standard of individual and group conduct as well as external factors, such as sustainable economic and ecologic strategies. Also, ethical accountability plays a progressively important role in academic fields.(https://en.wikipedia.org/wiki/Accountability)

Formative and Summative sampling –

Formative assessment is during the learning cycle where feedback is given to the learner, to be constructive and supportive in moving forward with progression.
http://www.education.gov.uk   states that "Assessment for learning takes place during learning, working with the learner to determine what is being learned and identifying what the 'next steps' are based on classroom practice where both the teachers and learners use feedback to improve learning"
Summative feedback is given at the end of a qualification to summarize the portfolio of work that has been submitted. It may require the learner to go

over and provide clearer evidence or competency over time.

The learner at this point will have completed his/her qualification, producing a portfolio of work in line with the criteria set out in the standards set by the awarding body for that qualification. The learner will be able to answer confidently any questions and demonstrate an understanding of what has been learnt, whilst undertaking this course. Greer (2007), states that summative assessment is the "after the teaching" sense to it. Thus, meaning that this is completed after the learner has learnt. This is also the point at which a learner may then have to take a final exam.

The key principles of IQA include:
SMART planning
Record keeping
Ethics
Equality and Diversity
CPD
Communication
Assessor competency

SMART planning – Specific targets are set for the learner, that can be measured by completion, in a timeframe that is achievable and realistic. Targets set are within the criteria of the qualification and support the learner in achieving personal learning and thinking skills.

Record keeping - There is a need to keep records of assessment so that there is an audit trail of the learner's journey showing progression and development of the learner. The teacher can refer to work produced and see how and what was planned from the previous session. Each learner / student is individual and so each plan will be unique, it will identify the learners development needs and progression through the course.

This is history of the learners journey through their qualification, things they are doing well and coping with, things they are struggling with, where they have been signposted for research and support, various websites and books. There are a variety of records that are kept:

1. Registration;
2. Administration;
3. ILP (individual Learning Plan);
4. Personnel file;
5. Records of assignments, and work, including action plans;
6. Records of achievement.

The requirements for keeping records of assessment are to prove achievement, track progress, and make sure all criteria is met and keeping record of attendance. There is also a legal requirement for funding and certification. Keeping records also shows a learners progression and achievement as a journey. There are boundaries and legislation regarding what can be collected and kept and how it can be used.

The Data Protection Act 1998 states that records must be kept securely, be relevant and not excessive, accurate and up to date and not kept for longer than necessary. Students can request a copy of all information held about them under the Freedom of Information Act 2000.

Internally the company keeps records because of policies and procedures set out, within the company, including performance indicators, statistics, student data, assessment tracking, grading of assessors.

Tummons (2011:74) states "I understand this very well and hence try to be as meticulous with paperwork as possible in my role" this is because it is better to have written correctly and sufficiently at the beginning.

External requirements, from awarding bodies, inspectors (OFSTED) legislation, funding bodies (SfA), and other professional bodies are to have the qualification handbook as a guide and reference for all qualifications, the awarding bodies, inspectors, and professional bodies will require a scheme of work, session plans, evidence of structured and planned approach to delivery of the subjects/sessions. Individual learning plans are kept as well to support claims for funding of learners.

All documents must be secured in order to maintain within legislation, regard the Data Protection Act 2003, which was amended from 1998, to include all electronic data.

Ethics - Ethics concern an individual's moral judgements about right and wrong. Decisions taken within an organisation may be made by individuals or groups, but whoever makes them will be influenced by the culture of the company. The decision to behave ethically is a moral one; employees must decide what they think is the right course of action. This may involve rejecting the route that would lead to the biggest short-term profit. Ethical behaviour and corporate social responsibility can bring significant benefits to a business. For example, they may:

Attract customers to the firm's products, thereby boosting sales and profits

Make employees want to stay with the business, reduce labour turnover and therefore increase productivity Attract more employees wanting to work for the business, reduce recruitment costs and enable the company to get the most talented employees Attract investors and keep the company's share price high, thereby protecting the business from takeover.

Unethical behaviour or a lack of corporate social responsibility, by comparison, may damage a firm's reputation and make it less appealing to stakeholders. Profits could fall as a result.

Follow link - http://businesscasestudies.co.uk/cadbury-schweppes/ethical-business-practices/the-importance-of-ethics-in-business.html#ixzz2WMemM6jd

Equality and Diversity – In everything a person does or says they have to be equal to all and diverse in their delivery. This is where we establish an understanding in the class of the types of people we are teaching and building rapport with, where we need to account for everyone's taste and communicate with all students regardless of their race, religion, culture, background, sexual origination or gender To include all students when teaching and teach in a style that accounts for Visual learners, by giving hand outs, for Audible learners, by speaking to them, and Kinaesthetic learners by getting them to do some activities. Allowing for flexibility in the activities so that all students can complete the tasks without being made to feel awkward, or stupid for taking longer than others To understand that some students have different needs and will take longer to achieve a task, allow for the person that completes tasks on time to go and help your student that is finding the task difficult, or to have an extension on the task given to allow for slower students.

CPD – Continuing Personal Development
This is where self assessment takes place; the IQA is checking that the assessor has kept their own development up to date, attending standardisation meetings, reading and keeping up to date with new developments in related industry, attending training sessions, internal or external to progress themselves. A CPD plan can be drawn up and

placed in with the rationale to demonstrate commitment to personal development.

Communication – Communication is the exchange and flow of information and ideas from one person to another, without this clear instruction there would be mistakes. This is essential between all staff members so that everyone has an understanding of their position and what they need to do and when.

"No one would talk much in society if they knew how often they misunderstood others". — Johann Wolfgang Von Goethe

Assessor competency – ensuring the assessor is experienced and competent in their role, maintaining and updating learning and development in their CPD records.
DEMONSTRATION OF ASSESSOR COMPETENCE

Assessors need to be competent in order to effectively plan and conduct assessments and report assessment results. An assessor's competence is based on the foundation provided by education, training and experience. Assessor competence is measured by the demonstration of the application of specific assessor knowledge, skills and personal attributes, as described in Section 2

Methods of demonstration and evaluation of assessor competence
Various methods may be used by accreditation bodies to evaluate the competence of assessors. These methods should be used in an appropriate combination to give the required level of confidence in assessor competence. Demonstration and evaluation of assessor competence include, but are not limited to the following methods:

Examination/testing/training evaluation
Written or oral examination may be used to determine an assessor's knowledge and skills (Section 2.2) as appropriate to the needs of the accreditation body.

Demonstration
The planned and formal witnessing of specific assessor skill performance, such as in role play situations.

Formal evaluation
The formal, planned and structured witnessing and evaluation of assessor performance during an actual assessment.

Casual observation
The unplanned, or informal witnessing of limited assessor performance. This observation could take

place in actual assessment or other situations in which assessment skills or personal attributes can be observed.

Documentation
This is all recorded information; such as resumes; assessment logs; training certificates; transcripts, certifications; and professional licenses.

Attestation
An attestation may give different levels of confidence depending on the credibility and independence of the provider. Either oral or written statement can be used as a testimonial.

Verification
An independent check or provision of additional objective evidence obtained to support other methods of evaluating competency, such as attestation and documentation.

Review of previous work
The review of assessor reports, completed checklists, assessment plans or other writing samples.

Interview
Interviews may involve one or more interviewers and the use of selection boards or evaluation panels. Interviews may also be used to verify evidence from other sources, and could provide

witness testimony/statement to the competency of the interviewee.

https://www.ilac.org/documents/ILAC_G11_07_2006_ILAC_guidelines_on_qualifications_and_competence_of_assessors.pdf

1.3The roles of practitioners involved in the internal and external quality assurance process

The IQA cycle will ensure the continually of assessment processes and evaluate to implement improvement. Records of this will be kept to provide an audit trail for regulatory authorities and awarding bodies.

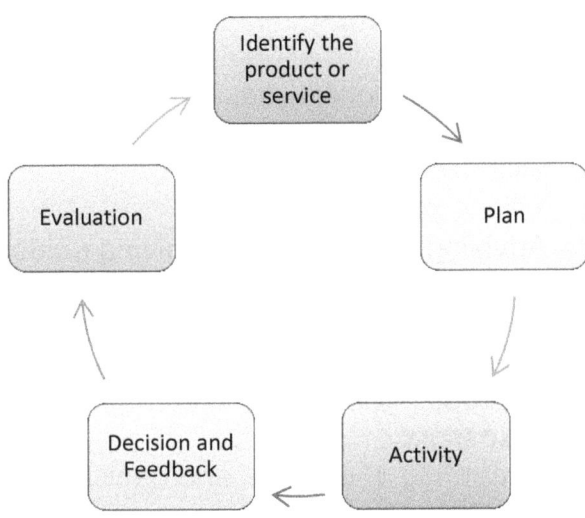

Identify the product or service
What is to be assessed and why, criteria needs to be clear.
Plan
Plan for who, what, where, when recording all planning events

Activity

Assess assessor competency in chosen criteria, according to the rationale.

Decision and Feedback

Has the assessor met the criteria for assessment, as planned, given constructive feedback on areas to develop, and recorded in IQA plan.

Evaluation

Evaluate areas of improvement and what needs to be reviewed or revisited.

The roles and responsibilities of practitioners are:

- Planning and carrying out sampling of assessed work
- Taking part in CPD
- Advising, supporting and giving guidance to assessors
- Providing constructive, developmental feedback
- Recording the quality assurance plan of assessors
- Recording of process and decisions within the plan
- To ensure that assessors understand and apply correct procedures
- Identify and issues or trends
- Interviewing learners, witnesses and managers
- Undertaking standardisation meetings
- Monitor and observe the learner journey from start to finish

1.4 The regulations and requirements for IQA in my own area of practice.

I have to follow company policies and procedures which include the following:
- VACSR assessment
- Appeals and complaints
- Confidentiality of information
- Data protection
- Copyright
- Equality and Diversity
- Health and Safety
- Welfare

There are also external regulation and legislation that I need to adhere to which are the following:
- The Data Protection Act
- The Health and Safety at Work Act
- The Equality Act
- Disability Discrimination Act

Copyright – make sure that any resources used are not copyright, protecting the learner, assessor, and organisation. Taken from http://www.cla.co.uk/copyright_information/copyright_information/ Copyright is one of the main types of intellectual property - others include designs, patents and trademarks. Intellectual property allows a person to own things they create in the same way as something physical can be owned. It is the right to prevent others copying or reproducing someone's work.

The main legislation dealing with copyright in the United Kingdom is the Copyright, Design and Patents Act, 1988

Welfare – to make sure that working environment is safe, the learner is comfortable in their role and has no issues, with the employer, the assessor or the work that has been undertaken.

2.1 The importance of planning and preparing IQA activities.

Planning and preparing is very important part of the IQA cycle. Planning will provide structure, and context for each assessment, what to observe and monitor, writing up a rational. When preparing a plan for formative and summative IV of assessor portfolios, allowing time for any actions to be corrected. The IQA will also build on a working knowledge of the assessor's competency in delivering each unit, allowing time for reflection and evaluation. Planning ahead will also structure developmental needs and training.

2.2 The components of an IQA plan
Within the rationale, there will be a copy of the assessors CV, and qualification certificates, this provides evidence of the assessors competency to deliver in these qualifications. The A1 award or equivalent, to show they are qualified, or a CPD log to show that they are to complete this award within

a 6 month timeframe. A record of meeting attended internally or externally to show standardisation has taken place.

The sampling plan its self will have the assessors name whether they are qualified or not, the name of the qualification, the unit number and the assessment method that is planned, and the assessment method that was carried out. A plan will look similar to this one below taken from http://www.cityandguilds.com/~/media/Documents/ ProvideTraining/Centre%20Document%20Library/Q uality-Assurance- documents/Guidance_on_Internal_Quality_Assuran ce_of_Qualifications_Forms_and_Documents.ashx

INTERNAL QUALITY ASSURANCE SAMPLING PLAN AND RECORD

Qualification: xxx **Standardisation unit:** Unit 1 (Communication) across all levels

Name of IQA: xxxxx

Assessor	Assessor Status	Assessment Site	Candidate	been assessed. Units to be sampled	Assessment process reviewed	Method of assessment checked
Karen x	Q	Chelmsford	William x	Ass. 1,2,3 Sam 4,5	P/R/F	DO/WP
Mark y	Q	Braintree	Alison	Ass 1,2,3,4 ,5,Sam 6,7,8	P/R/F	EWT/WT
Jack z	NSNQ	Witham	Gary	Ass – Sam 1,2,3,4	P/R/F	DO/Q

Assessor Status Key

Q – Qualified
NQ – Not Qualified
NSQ – New staff qualified
NSNQ – New staff not qualified
Assessment Process P – Planning R – Review F – Feedback FC – Final Check
Method of Assessment DO – Direct Observations RPL – Recognition of Prior Learning EWT – Expert Witness Testimony WP – Work Product WT – Witness Testimony Q – Questions APCS – Assignment / Project / Case Study S – Simulation

Also for a new assessor not qualified there should be some form to identify the person who is countersigning for the new assessor.
There is guidance for IQA on the city and guilds website, at the link above. I have printed this booklet, as reference for myself.

2.3 The practical preparations that need to be made for IQA

Preparations needed for Internal Quality Assurance	
Collect Information	Before going out I need to know where I am going and with whom, who the learner is on site and the qualification they are doing. What units have already been sampled, what units need to be sampled, what assessment methods I need to cover, do I have all the paperwork I need for the day. Is the assessor qualified or not.

Communications	I need to make sure that the assessor knows I am coming out with them; I need to be told which site I am going to and who I am there to see. I need to make sure the assessor is aware of the assessment methods I will be using. I need to make sure that plans have been recorded and I have all paperwork I need
Admin Arrangements	I have all legal forms I need to fill in and know the process of recording and storing these.
Resources	Paperwork for on site, ability to get to site at arranged time. Laptop, dongle for internet if needed.

3.1 <u>Evaluate different techniques for evidence sampling of assessments including use of technology</u>

Direct Observations	This is a good way to see the ability of the student, to assess their competency in a task, and to be able to give feedback directly, or support them in correcting the task they are doing. Assessors that are new to the role, may be nervous when being watched whilst working with a learner, therefore more likely to make silly mistakes; and so it is the duty of the IQA to put the assessor at ease before this can be achieved. This is an excellent opportunity to assess firsthand the assessors ability and understanding in natural surroundings, having to adapt to possible changes, as they happen and to deal with unforeseen circumstances.
Recognition of Prior Learning	This will be discussed at the beginning, such as the initial assessment where the IQA will establish the competency of

	the assessor in their delivery, having a CV and certificates of qualification achievements, when looking to forward plan for CPD and standardisation
Work Product	The IQA will be looking at written and verbal feedback; they will also be looking at the quality of feedback and clear evidence of signposting, action plans, and the learners' journey, as well as learning and teaching that has taken place. It is important that the assessor is aware that all work based learning requires at least 51% teaching and 49% assessment
Questions	Questions will make the assessor think about the answer and draw on knowledge, as well as an understanding for the topic, may also clarify once spoken aloud Some assessor when new to the role, will be nervous about giving answers in case they are incorrect, so may not volunteer to answer or mumble/stutter as not

	confident. I feel that this is the best way to gauge an understanding and competency of an assessor's knowledge and ability.

3.2 Explain the appropriate criteria to use for judging the quality of the assessment process

The criteria is set in the form of questions, used to judge the assessor on the quality of the process the questionnaire will be something similar to this:

IQA Observation and Questioning Checklist:

Did the Assessor:
Develop and agree an assessment plan with the learner(s) using appropriate assessment methods?
Agree when assessment will take place with learner(s) and other people involved?
Agree arrangements with the learner(s) for reviewing progress against the assessment plan?
Review and update assessment plans to take account of learner achievements?
Give the learner(s) feedback at an appropriate time and pace?

Give feedback in a constructive and encouraging way?
Give feedback to the learner(s) which met their needs and was appropriate to their level of confidence?
Clearly explain the assessment decisions?
Encourage learner(s) to get advice on the assessment decisions?

Can the Assessor explain?
How to operate the centre standardisation and internal quality assurance procedures?
How to access the centre appeals and access to fair assessment policy?
What information is made available by the awarding organisation and QAC?
How to identify and gain resources to support learners who have special assessment needs?
This observation and questioning sheet will vary in different training providers, but cover the questions that are laid out her, as this is guidance for all centres from City and Guilds.

4.1 Summarize the types of feedback, support, and advice that assessors may need to maintain and improve on the quality of assessment.

Feedback, Support and Advice for the improvement on Quality of Assessment	
Feedback – from the Assessor to the learner Observations of this can support the Assessor – the same feedback can apply from IQA to the assessor as given for assessor to learner.	The feedback given during assessment must be constructive and supportive. Before giving feedback make sure you remind yourself why you are doing it. The purpose for giving feedback is to improve the situation or performance. You won't accomplish that by being harsh, critical, or offensive. That's not to say you must always be positive. There is a role for negativity and even anger if someone isn't paying sufficient attention to what you're saying. However this should be used sparingly. You'll most often get much more from people when your approach is positive and focused on improvement. http://www.mindtools.com/pages/article/newTMM_98.htm
Feedback – from	By involving the manager/mentor that is supporting the learner, the learner

Mentor/ Manager Again this can apply to the IQA as support from the Assessors Line Manager will support them in their role.	will feel motivated and have someone onsite that they can turn to for immediate support.
Feedback from Peers	Involving colleagues can be beneficial if they are also completing a qualification – they can support each other as long as boundaries set out include clear guidelines around plagiarism.
Feedback – Self Evaluation	This supports the learner with their Personal Learning and Thinking Skills (PLTS) it helps them to identify their training and development needs and helps them to understand how other people may view them in a different way, with self evaluation the learner is usually quite hard on themselves.
Support – signposting	When an Assessor is unable to support or advice the learner, it is good practice to see signposting,

IQA to Assessor – this can also apply in this role	recorded on action plans. It also shows that the assessor has knowledge of where to get support if they are unable to help the learner. Signposting is a form of directing the learner to other support centres.
Support – resources IQA will have resources to support the Assessor and should be prepared to support the Assessor when on site / observations	An Assessor should plan, prior to a site visit with the candidate, therefore they should be aware of the needs of the learner and have resources to hand to support them, as an example, if the internet were unavailable at the time, them it would be good practice for the assessor to have some type of paper resource that would support the learner. Resources can be anything that promotes learning and engages students.
Support – Advice IQA to Assessor – the Assessor should be aware that	An Assessor can only advice on what they know and so depending on the subject will be dependent on their knowledge, which is when signposting is important.

the IQA is always on hand to give advice where possible.	

4.2 Explain standardization requirements in relation to assessment

The process should consider the external influences that have an impact on the assessment, such as Awarding Bodies, H&S, and qualification criteria. The qualification aims and the criteria required to meet those aims. The methods of assessment taking place for individual units and best practice to meet the standards. The methods of teaching and learning that lead to best practice. Feedback methods and marking of work products, written questions, reflective accounts, case studies etc... Therefore the IQA team will have set benchmarks to adhere to within codes of practice, policies and procedures. They will monitor the support given to the assessor, and the assessors' ability to manage their teaching and support to the learners. The IQA is also responsible for arranging meetings with the assessors and their learners, for observation and monitoring of teaching and learning that is taking place. Regular meetings will ensure that best practice is set as standard across the rest of the team. All assessment practices should be standardized across the company, so that all assessments meet the standards for VACRS.

4.3 Explain relevant procedures regarding disputes about the quality of assessment

Any dispute over the quality of assessment should be feedback to the Lead verifier. There is a form, IQA concerns, and this needs to be filled in with details of the area/s for concern, the agreed actions to take and the time in which to complete. This form will be signed by the IQA and the IQA counter signer (if necessary). There will then be a review in which the agreed actions discussed and complete the form with the action taken, once all is complete the form is then signed by the IQA and Lead verifier

5.1 Evaluate requirements for information management, data protection, and confidentiality in relation to the IQA of assessment.

The following was taken from the IQA Guidance Handbook (City and Guilds)
All IQAs are required to implement the policies and procedures of their own organisation and those of the awarding organisation. This may be in relation to areas such as secure transport and storage of learner work, maintaining confidentiality, implementing the requirements for data protection etc. In addition IQAs are responsible for ensuring that all team members carry out their responsibilities in relation to legislation. In particular this includes requirements for: health, safety and welfare and equality issues including bilingualism. IQAs should check that all requirements continue to be met as part of the ongoing monitoring carried out in the centre. The IQA also has a supporting role by creating and maintaining complete and up to date records of information is a particularly important function. When the centre is inspected, audited or monitored by an external agency, the following range of information will need to be made available:

The written IQA procedures
• Numbers of current registered learners per qualification and level
• Learner centre enrolment and awarding organisation registration details

• Tutor and assessor details – specifically CVs, CPD records, assessor qualifications (A1, V1 or relevant TAQA units), development plans and workloads
• Learner progress reviews and achievements, special assessment requirements and equal opportunities monitoring information
• Training programmes, assessment records, plans, reviews and tracking sheets
• Available learner support resources
• Details of learning and assessment sites
• Details of satellite, franchise or partnership arrangements
• The internal quality assurance sampling strategy
• IQA records including feedback to tutors, assessors, discussions with learners
• Records of claims for certification
• Learner work and/or portfolios
• Minutes of internal quality assurance meetings Records of standardisation activities
• Procedures for storage and retention of centre records

Following activity by the external quality assurer there is a real need to promptly disseminate information. In some centres any action points are agreed with a programme co-ordinator or qualification managers then individual IQAs have responsibility to communicate pertinent parts of the external quality assurer's report to those tutors and assessors for whom they are responsible.

It is important that action points raised by the external quality assurer are acted upon within the timescales specified. Failure to do so may result in a high risk rating as specified in the 'Our Quality Assurance Requirements'. Because of security implications, it is extremely important that no claims for certification are made without the clearance of the IQA for the qualification. It is not acceptable for any claim for certification to be made by an IQA who does not meet the requirements specified in the qualification strategy– this may include holding an appropriate qualification. Of equal importance is the need to maintain security of learner work and their assessment records.

Work and portfolios for learners who have been certificated in between external quality assurer activities must be kept intact until the next activity so that they can be examined if requested. Original assessment records must be retained for at least three years and be made available for external quality assurance and to allow for any appeals or complaints to be progressed and resolved.

6.1 Evaluate legal issues, policies and procedures relevant to the IQA of assessment including those for health and safety, and welfare.

Question 5.1 covered legalities regarding paperwork.

When an IQA visit takes place the IQA is looking to see that the learner and the assessor are working in a safe environment, checking that the assessor is aware of the surroundings and the risks.

Quality and quality assurance measures need to be built into all processes in the 'learner journey' these include the:

• Recruitment process
• Induction process
• Initial assessment
• Learning plans
• Teaching
• Facilitating learning
• Reviews of progress
• Assessment processes
• Achievement
• Progression planning

Taking all these points into account will monitor the safe working environment and welfare of the learner, during recruitment there will be a discussion around the learner and their role, which will identify any health and safety factors to consider. During induction, again health and safety will be discussed and monitored throughout. When drawing up learning plans after initial assessment there may be a need for training, which can be incorporated into the learners work by teaching or training, by the assessor or in-house.

You also need to ensure that you consider legislation and policies related to the welfare of all assessors, such as planning their assessor allocation so they are able to manage their workloads without undue stress.

There needs to be good communication between team members to avoid team members working in isolation. Even if there is an Internal Quality Assurance Coordinator taking overall responsibility for the coordination of the quality assurance team, each IQA/IV needs to report back their findings on a regular basis.

6.2 <u>Evaluate different ways in which technology can contribute to the IQA of assessment</u>.

Technology now impacts on every aspect of life to an extent. It is quite likely that most of the candidates, assessors and IQA staff will have mobile phones or personal organizers with internet access and the means to take videos, record sound and take photos. Some will be able to use Skype features. All candidates, assessors and IQA staff will have computer access, some being provided in the workplace, but also being able to book time in college learning centres, training centres or libraries. Having this technology is a benefit to assessors to record and reference into portfolios that are now also on line. The IQA is made easier for formative and summative assessment by having electronic data to be able to assess the work of the assessor with different qualifications / units and learners in one place. The benefits to the assessor are that they no longer physically need to produce the work at a set time, as electronic data is accessible 24/7. This does not mean that the IQA processes and procedures should be placed aside, but this technology can be used to enhance the IQA process with electronic formatted paperwork, that can be filled out on the laptop, no longer printed and sent but, attached to an email to transfer over to others, involved in the IQA process, and therefore making the working life of the IQA easier.

6.3 Explain the value of reflective practice and CPD in relation to IQA

This is where an assessor would write about or talk about a situation that has happened, specific to an area that needs to be covered. Reflecting on what happened and if they could have done anything different this will be in the assessor own wording and will be how they viewed an experienced or situation. This is best to be recorded on DVR where you can ask questions to draw out more knowledge or clarify the assessors understanding.

Gibbs (1988) model of reflection, although based on health care can be adapted to use in any situation to help when writing a reflective account. I use the model of reflection as a guidance tool. This helps to produce an assessors training plan and when reviewed regularly can be used to produce an assessors learning and development plan to help the assessor to continually develop them.

6.4 Evaluate requirements for equality and diversity and, where appropriate, bilingualism, in relation to the IQA of assessment.

Centres will often have targets to meet, set in response to government initiatives. Here is an example:

- A centre wants to increase the percentage of female or ethnic minority candidates on particular courses to mirror the percentage of those groups in the local population.

The internal quality assurance process will need to take such targets into account.
Data on registrations could be fed back to those responsible for marketing and publicity, and data on progression needs to be shared with assessors and other IVs, as well as teaching or training teams, if these comprise different staff.

Other examples might be:
 1. The allocation of assessors of a particular gender – for example, in some health and social care situations; arrangements that take in to the personal needs of candidates and assessors;
2. Sensitivity to religious and cultural backgrounds, eg planning assessments and internal quality assurance to avoid holidays and religious festivals;
 3. Ensuring requests for support in cases of dyslexia, bilingualism or a need for translators are within requirements.
Taken from
http://my.safaribooksonline.com/book/career-development/9780749461652

Bibliography

http://www.journeytoexcellence.org.uk/videos/expertspeakers/assessmentstrategiesdylanwiliamtrans.asp

www.anngravell.co.uk

https://en.wikipedia.org/wiki/Accountability

https://www.ilac.org/documents/ILAC_G11_07_2006_ILAC_guidelines_on_qualifications_and_competence_of_assessors.pdf

http://www.cla.co.uk/copyright_information/copyright_information/

http://www.cityandguilds.com/~/media/Documents/ProvideTraining/Centre%20Document%20Library/Quality-Assurance-

documents/Guidance_on_Internal_Quality_Assuran
ce_of_Qualifications_Forms_and_Documents.ashx

http://www.cityandguilds.com/~/media/Documents/Provi
deTraining/Centre%20Document%20Library/Quality-
Assurance-
documents/Guidance_on_Internal_Quality_Assurance_
of_Qualifications_Forms_and_Documents.ashx

http://www.mindtools.com/pages/article/newTMM_98.ht
m

http://my.safaribooksonline.com/book/career-
development/9780749461652

Milton Keynes UK
Ingram Content Group UK Ltd.
UKHW021313070724
445287UK00024B/269